AF446554

Holy Whispers

Cry Out . . . and Listen!

JOY A. EMERY-GULDEN

ISBN 979-8-89112-318-2 (Paperback)
ISBN 979-8-89112-320-5 (Hardcover)
ISBN 979-8-89112-319-9 (Digital)

Copyright © 2024 Joy A. Emery-Gulden
All rights reserved
First Edition

All rights reserved. No part of this publication may be reproduced, distributed, or transmitted in any form or by any means, including photocopying, recording, or other electronic or mechanical methods without the prior written permission of the publisher. For permission requests, solicit the publisher via the address below.

Covenant Books
11661 Hwy 707
Murrells Inlet, SC 29576
www.covenantbooks.com

To my Lord, my Jesus, who called me to be
His own when I was just a small child;
To my late husband, John, and my
granddaughter, Mykaela, who have already
passed through the thin veil that separates
us—to a new and beautiful afterlife;
and to my beautiful family;
They have written indelible stories on my heart!

INTRODUCTION

Years ago, I was sitting in church. Right before the service started, the assistant minister's wife slipped in beside me. She leaned over and whispered that she was in charge of the music for a women's retreat on prayer in about a month. She asked me if I would help her. I said, "Yes."

I went home that day and said to myself, "Joy, what were you thinking?" I hadn't even said that I would think about it. I just said, "Yes." At the time, I was raising a family and working full-time. My only days off were Saturday and Sunday. I had just volunteered to give up those days!

I did go to the retreat. Some things I learned there forever changed the way I will view prayer! I learned that listening is as much a part of prayer as talking to God. I also started to keep a journal of some prayers I have prayed and words God has spoken to me.

I have learned that in the busyness of life, I need to find time to be silent, to take a few minutes out of a busy day to sit with Jesus and let Him restore my soul. I need to be sincere. Prayer is just being genuine, honest, and real with God. It is just talking with God about how things really are. It's coming to God with no agenda, just the way I am.

One of the most important things I need is to be thankful! I have been blessed with *so* much! I am rich compared to so much of the world. I have a new day to live! One of the first things I aim to do each day is to get down on my knees and thank God for giving me the gift of another day!

I am also learning to stop making prayer all about me. I come to God with my list of all the things I want or think I need, but shouldn't prayer be all about God?

After that retreat, I started by reading a few portions of Scripture and then just being quiet, journaling, and writing down my thoughts. King Solomon, one of the richest and wisest men who ever lived, in Ecclesiastes 5:1–2, said, "Guard your steps when you go to the house of God. Go near to listen… Do not be hasty in your heart to utter anything before God. God is in heaven, you are on earth, so let your words be few."

When we are silent, sincere, and honest, and when we take time to listen, we learn life-changing truths. We are given inspiring thoughts and ideas that can even change the course of history. We find answers to life's dilemmas. Sometimes the answers we are looking for are right before our eyes.

Sometimes it is hard for us to pray, especially when we go through dark times. I pray that God's Spirit will use these words to bless you, to help give you words when you cannot pray and hear what His Spirit is saying to you.

Oh, God!

When I was in the depth of darkness and pain…
I did not want to love.
I did not want to feel.
I did not want to hear or see.
I did not want to kneel before You.
Everything was cold and dark. My strength was gone!
But there, in the darkness, Your hand reached down and touched my soul. Your arms held me near. That still, small whisper was Your voice saying, **"My child, do not fear. I am here! Let Me pour the healing oil of My Spirit over each tender wound. The petals of your wounded soul *will* bloom again.**

For now…
I will love for you!
I will feel for you!
I will hear your cry and see your tears!
I will kneel beside you and wash your weary feet!
Your darkness will give way to new dawning!
Joy, precious joy will come to you in the morning!"

Dear Jesus, my Friend,

A friend is someone who takes the shadows of your life and makes them sing...
Who takes the dark and ugly parts of you and sees beyond them to the beautiful...
Who gives when you do not ask...
Who stands beside you when you do not deserve it...
Who prays for you when you do not even know it...
Who stands before the Father in your place.
A friend's touch is a treasure, something miraculous...
Like soft snowflakes falling on your arm, each with a beauty all its own. A friend is a blessing, one who never gives up on you...
One who loves you just the way you are. Oh, Jesus, I am so blessed!
I have found this friend in You!

My dear, dear child,

I am **your Friend. I am the friend that sticks closer than a brother or sister.**

Even now, I am showering you with blessings your eyes may not even see. Open the eyes of your spirit. *See* **Me! Receive from Me!**

I am your Provider; I am your Strength when the days grow long. I will fulfill your needs and grant your desires. What I do for you is more than you can dream or imagine!

You see the temporary things. I see the eternal. Just walk with Me. Just rest in Me. Just seek Me. Just love Me.

I am the Friend who is your Very Great Reward. I am the Friend who is your Healer. I am the Friend who is your Life and Breath!

Come near to Me. Sit with Me. Linger here with Me. Worship Me.

Friends forever**!**

—John 15:15; Ephesians 3:20; Genesis 15:1

Holy Father,

By Your hand—yes, Your hand alone—I exist in this world. *You* breathe. That sweet breath fills my soul!

Your majestic fingers paint each stroke of the sunset with breathless beauty! I can only pause in the stillness of silent wonder!

That same strong hand reaches out to hold mine. Trembling, I grasp and hold on so tightly, surrendering to Your sweet, loving care.

How could I ever live without You? I would only be groping in the darkness of vast aloneness.

I will choose Your tender touch. Only You bestow life, yes, aliveness in my soul!

Your sweet, gentle Spirit descends on me, and heaven itself comes down!

You truly are the strength of my life—my hope forever!

Where would I go? You alone have captured my heart! I rest in you alone!

Oh, My child,

I am your life! I am your breath! I am the lifter of your head! I will satisfy the longing of your heart. I will pour out My Spirit on you and your offspring. I will use you to bring life and healing to many. Blessing—I will bless you. Multiplying—I will multiply you. I am here to be your God! I am here to be your Shepherd! I am here to walk with you. I will never leave you or forsake you. I am your strength. I am your peace. I will lead you beside quiet waters and restore your soul. Goodness and mercy will be yours, following you all the days of your life!

—Psalm 3:3; Psalm 23; Genesis 22:17; Psalm 59:9; John 16:33

Dear Jesus,

I want to worship You. I want to give my love and adoration to You. You are my Father, who loves and cares for me, and You accept me just the way I am. "Awesome" does not begin to describe You.

I am like a child, reaching out to You to be loved, to be held in Your strong arms, to be soothed when I am hurting.

Sometimes I have trouble picturing You as a loving Father. I can't feel what it is to be loved unconditionally by a father who truly cares.

I know You want to deliver me and heal me from so many things: the curse of words spoken against me, the pain of loss and rejection, the fear of not being accepted. When I am wounded, I want to cover it up so it will not hurt again. You want to dig open my wounds and pull out the weeds. Oh, how it will hurt!

I know You want to come then and pour Your healing oil over me. You want to heal me and set me free. Then I will be able to worship You with all my heart.

So with trembling hands and heart, I reach out and say, "Yes." Please come and do Your work in me. Take the broken and jagged pieces of my soul. Only You can make them into something beautiful—*You*, only *You*!

Oh, My child,

I long for you to come to Me and sit with Me in the stillness. Let the world pass us by frantic, hustling, worrying, running, pacing to and fro, spending restless energy chasing after what does not satisfy.

In the beauty of the silence, let Me satisfy your soul with My goodness and mercy. Let Me wash you clean in My forgiveness. Let Me open the eyes of your heart with praise and adoration. No need for words. My Spirit engulfs your spirit, and we are one.

Release yourself to Me, and I will release you from the pressure to succeed. I alone know your deepest needs and desires. I have gone ahead and charted your journey. I am your guide. Rest here awhile with Me. Let Me be your Way, your Truth, and your Light!

—Psalm 23; Psalm 46:10; John 14:6

Thank You, Jesus…

    …for being my rock when I am shaken, for being my defender when I have no more strength to fight; for being my forever when all I can do is walk through today; for being my strength when I can no longer stand; for carrying me when all I am able to take is one faltering step…

    …for loving me when I feel unloved and forsaken; for being my healer when all I know is brokenness; for reaching out and *touching* me when everyone else pushes away; for being my Light when I grope in the darkness; for being my song when I cannot sing; for being my friend when I feel all alone; for being my air when I cannot breathe; for holding onto me when I can't hold on any longer; for being my rainbow after the rain…

    …for sending the birds to sing over me; for pulling the weeds from my heart that choke out new growth; for walking with me in the morning in the fresh falling dew; for calling my name in the evening in the cool of the day; for opening up blue skies after the rain; for catching my tears pouring down on the dry earth; for flowers springing up all around me…

    …for forgiving me when I can't forgive myself, for being the sun shining in my face when I stand in the shadows of fear; for riding on the heavens to help me and on the clouds in Your *majesty*; for holding my face in Your hands, tenderly gazing at me with *love* in Your eyes; for receiving my praise when all I can do is lift up empty hands; for preparing the way ahead of me when I struggle to take one more step; for speaking to me in that still, small voice when the loudness of life tries to drown You out; for restoring my soul; for Your goodness and mercy that follow me all the days of my life; for new beginnings; for making new wine out of the crushed grapes of my soul…

…for family and friends who surround me and faith-fully hold me up in their prayers; for hearing my prayers when all I can do is weep and whisper…

…for *this moment* in Your presence! Amen.

Oh, My child,

My great delight is to care for you! I know your needs before you even cry out. I hear the cries of My righteous ones, and I come to deliver you. I will truly supply all that you need! The things that seem large and insurmountable to you are so small in My sight! I only have to speak the word, and it is done!

I desire for you to trust Me with the great things and with the small. I am your *Father,* and I do provide for the needs of My children.

All I ask is that you *trust*; trust in Me!

—Philippians 4:5-6,13

Dear Jesus,

You are my Prince of Peace. You come for me. You desire to take my hand. You put aside who I was and where I came from. You want to share with me everything in Your kingdom!

I have a choice. I can sit in my ashes in the corner and say, "No, I'm just a cinder girl. I'm not good enough for You!" Or I can take Your hand and leave the past behind, just go with You and be Your bride forever!

I see the walls standing between You and me and all the blessings You have for me—walls I have built!

You say, "The truth will set me free! Come, all who are weary and burdened, and I will give you rest!"

I don't want to live like this anymore: fearful, doubting, afraid to step out onto the waters! Today, I choose to leave the past behind, to lay my cares and burdens at Your feet and follow You—one step at a time!

My child,

Rest with Me here. Right now, that is all I am asking of you. Come away and rest awhile.

Rest your body, soul, mind and spirit. I know your desire is to serve Me, but you are not strong enough right now.

Rest, so I can strengthen you. Feast on My Words. Drink deeply from the living water I provide. I will strengthen you. I will help you. Let Me go before you. Rest on the pillow of My peace. Let My joy be your strength.

My purposes in you will be accomplished in *My* time. I am in you, and *I am all the strength you need*!

—**Psalm 91:1; Philippians 4:13**

Jesus,

Oh, Son of Righteousness, shine on me! Let me feel the healing in Your wings! Oh, Breath of Heaven, breathe on me with sweet wisps of all encircling grace.

Oh, Rose of Sharon, bloom in me. Open wide within my soul Your fragrance sweet! Oh, Bread of Heaven, feed me until I desire You more than any earthly food!

Oh, Lamb of God, my gentle Shepherd, lead me to Your ever-flowing springs of living water!

Oh, Prince of Peace, calm and soothe me until my soul is freed from every doubt and fear.

Oh, Heavenly Bridegroom, come for me. Oh, make me worthy to walk with You in white!

My child,

I am the Light that shines on your pathway. When you walk with Me, you are not walking in darkness. I can see what is ahead, and I know the way you should go. Nothing is hidden from My eyes.

I will be your guide. I am your hidden treasure. Treasure My Words more than your necessary food. Treasure Me more than the air you breathe, more than your life itself.

I am yours, and you are Mine. I am the light of your life. I am the creator of your days. Trust Me. Love Me. Live in Me. Follow Me. Obey Me. Is that too much to ask?

I gave My life for you!

—John 8:12; Job 23:12; Psalm 32:8

Dear Lord,

Sometimes it seems like You are so far away; I can't feel You. My faith says, "Hold on. I know He's got to be here walking with me." I can only stand on Your Word that says You will *never* leave me or forsake me. Thank You.

Oh, lift the cloud that has settled over me and weighed me down. I want to see You in Your spender and holiness—pure, shining, beautiful. I am reaching out to *You*!

I need You. Help me see to follow in Your footsteps, though the silence deafens me! Show me the way I should go as I lift up my soul to You!

Breathe Your peace upon me. Hide me in the shadow of Your wings. Hold me close. I rest in You.

I choose to worship You!

My child,

Draw near, and I will spread My tent over you. My banner over you is *love*!

I have set you apart for Myself and My purposes. Walk in faith. Do not fear. Don't look back!

I know the plans I have for you—plans not to harm you but to prosper you, to give you hope and a future. I only ask that you follow hard after Me!

Open the ears of your heart and receive My words. I am speaking to your soul in gentle whispers. Look only to Me. I will show you the way to go as you lift up your soul to Me.

Your praises warm My heart! My peace is surrounding you! With safety, I encircle you. I hem you in behind and before and rest My hand on you.

—Song of Songs 2:4; Revelation 7:15; Jeremiah 29:11; Psalm 143:8; Psalm 32:7; Psalm 139:5

Thank You, Jesus…

...that You love me.

Your love for me does not depend on what I do or say, what I don't do or don't say. Earthly love is so conditional. Your love for me is based on total acceptance of who I am and who You created me to be. It surrounds me like a warm blanket. It does not judge or demand perfection. It only is—eternally is—so deep You traded Your life for mine.

You took the blame for all my sins, my imperfections, my mistakes, my unkind thoughts and words, the lies I have spoken to myself, and You washed me in this love. *You* set me free!

If I could only begin to comprehend such a love, my soul would sing forever in the rapture of You—just You, only You!

Oh, My child,

My tender love flows over you as I hold you gently in My arms. My heart is warmed when you praise Me. My Spirit is truly intertwined with yours. The sweetness of your praise fills My heart with joy! Tenderness surrounds our love.

Oh, let *My* joy be your strength, *My* love be your portion, *My* life give new life to your soul and spirit!

Walk straightly in the pathway of My love. Do not turn to the right or to the left, only follow with passion the course I have laid out for you. I will go before you and make the crooked places straight.

—Nehemiah 8:10; Proverbs 4:27; Isaiah 45:2

Jesus,

From You I draw my everything! From You I draw my strength. From You and You alone I draw my breath—the breath that gives me life. Without You I am nothing.

My heart's desire is to please You. It pains me so when I fall short. But You extend Your hand of mercy and work in me the things I cannot do alone.

I desire a pure heart. I desire clean hands. I desire to be able to bask in Your presence, far away from the cares of this life.

Help me to focus on the eternal, but give me wisdom for the temporary here and now. May my life be a gentle, fragrant offering to You.

May I always be able to see the prints of Your footsteps and follow in them…close to You, the One I love.

My child,

You shall truly know My mind as you search for Me with all your heart, as you hunger for Me with all your soul, as you thirst for Me with all that is in you. I delight to reveal Myself to you.

Seek Me in the simple places as well as in the great. Hear Me in the gentle whispers as well as in the deep revelations. Let My words grow deep into your heart and soul and become so much a part of you that whether you are awake or asleep, My words will flow within your spirit.

My wisdom is as a bottomless ocean: vast, immeasurable, deep, high and wide. Day by day, moment by moment, seek...and you *will* find!

—Jeremiah 29:13; Psalm 46:10;
Proverbs 16:22; Matthew 7:7

Dear Lord,

You are beautiful beyond description. I desire to be one with You. I desire for You to let Your love permeate my soul so that You can bear Your fruit in me. May all those around me be blessed.

Oh, may I be like that tree growing with my roots down deep in You, satisfied with the rain of Your Spirit, the goodness and warmth of Your sunshine. I cannot bear fruit on my own. I want to let You bear Your sweet fruit in me.

And I will lift up my branches in praise to You, the Almighty, the glorious One!

My child,

I long for you. Come, lay your head on My shoulder. Let Me hold you close. Rest from the busyness of this world.

Let Me sing My quiet songs over you. Let Me surround you with My love and mercy. Let Me restore your soul.

The world knows no peace. I give you a peace that no one but a child of Mine can understand.

Empty your heart and mind of the cares and burdens of the day. I am your Father. I long to do good for you.

Lay your cares here at My feet. In exchange, I breathe My peace on you.

—Zephaniah 3:17; Psalm 23; John 14:27

Dear Lord,

I hear Your voice saying, "Come!" The waves are beating, and the wind is loud. I'm having trouble seeing You. I want to step out of the boat and walk on the waters of Your plans for me, but I don't know which way to go. Are You saying, "Wait!" or "Step out now!"

Please clear the mist of my anxious thoughts, my confusion, and the frantic beating of my heart. Help me see clearly! If I can only see a glimpse of You or hear what direction Your voice is coming from, I will step out and walk with You on the waters of Your plans for me.

I hear too many echoes.

Lord, I know You are calling me. And I say, "Yes, Lord, yes!" I will walk with You! I will ride with You! I will sail the seas with You! I will sit quietly with You!

Please give me the strength that I need to surrender. Wash me in the blood of the Lamb. Purify me like gold. Clothe me in white.

Oh, may I be a reflection of You to this dying world!

My child,

I hear you. I have your future in My strong hands. I know your heart and your desire to follow Me.

You have been so concerned about material things. I am concerned about eternal things.

Moments, hours, days all run together. There are no finites of time where I live. I am the beginning all the way to the end. You are in the middle now. Strive to press on. Do not give in to fear or inadequacy. Do not fix your eyes on the storm but on *Me*!

I am reaching for your hand. There is power in My touch: power to rescue, power to save, power to deliver, power to transform, and power to renew! Grab hold of My hand, and do not let go! We will walk across the waters together. You will not sink. You will not suffer defeat.

I am your strength! *You* are strong *only* when you walk with Me!

—Matthew 14:25-32

Jesus,

You, who, with one word, "Peace," silenced the storm, hushed the waves, silence my turbulent thoughts, my worried heart, my desperate grasping to have my own way!

You, who, with a touch opened blind eyes, open mine that I may see You again for the first time—new and glorious, powerful, perfect, and beautiful!

You, who gave back hearing to the deaf, open my ears that I may hear Your voice in the cool of the day, walking in the garden of my heart, longing for me to walk with You, longing for my companionship. May I never be too busy to hear You calling me. Help me listen for Your quiet footsteps! I will take Your hand and walk with You!

You, who turned water into the best of wine, turn my ordinary into immeasurably more by Your precious Spirit.

You, who called forth, and the dead came to life, call out from me all that is dying, wretched, barren, and waste. Help me come alive in You!

You, who died a criminal's death but were the epitome of innocence and righteousness, make me willing to die to all that is not of You, to give *my* life for You, follow You down any road whatever the cost!

You, who rose triumphant…

You, who hold the keys of death and hell…

You, who live and reign forever…

breathe in me new life! Help me know You more and love You more. Empower me to reach out with this gift of life to all who are entrapped in unlit holes of despair.

Jesus, help me every day to never lose sight of who You are: *King of kings, Lord of lords, the only true God, the supreme ruler of the universe, the God-man, the healer, the deliverer, the rescuer and my God and my King!*

My precious child,

I hear your prayers as you offer them up to Me. I delight in answering you, even as a father delights in giving precious gifts to his children.

My ways are much higher than your ways. I do not always answer in the ways you expect. I want only what is best for you. I can see the way ahead of you clearly. Be still before Me. Quiet your heart. Listen for My voice. In quietness and confidence is your strength.

I am answering, but do you hear Me? Wisdom sometimes passes with quiet footsteps. Only those attuned to My presence can acquire her. Only those who seek will find!

—Isaiah 55:9; Isaiah 30:15; Proverbs 3

Jesus,

Sweet are these moments beholding Your face. Sweet is the taste of Your words and Your grace. Sweet is the touch of Your hand on my brow.

Sweet is the healing You bring to me now.

The breath of heaven touches me gently—sweet wind of Your presence—refreshing my soul, making me whole, wholly Yours!

Come with Your spring rains. Wash away life's debris, cluttering what would be fertile soil.

Warm Sonshine, Light of lights, shine Your pure and holy rays on me. Warm my body, soul, mind, and spirit with Your healing radiance. Open up the petals of my soul. May they be fragrant and beautiful as I reach up to You, the Son!

As birds announce the coming of spring, sing Your pure, sweet songs to my heart. May all the cold, harsh blunders of my soul and all that would pain Your inmost being lie in death's sleep under the whiteness of Your crimson flow.

Even as the crocus pushes up through the snow in the spring, may I be resurrected in newness of the life You breathe on me. May I spring forth in rainbow colors—radiant, pure, and sweet—glorifying You, the Son!

Oh, My child,

Come sit at My feet, and let Me love you. Let Me just hold you in My strong arms. Don't rush away.

Let My words sink down deep into your soul.

In the stillness, sense My glory, My grace, My unconditional love! Stay here with Me for a while. Let your heart rest, away from the cares and worries of this day.

Free your mind from the burdens and weary things. Let Me illumine your whole self with the light of life and peace…My peace.

Let not your heart be troubled, and don't be afraid! You believe in God. Believe also in Me. I am here. *I AM!*

—Matthew 11:28–29; John 14:1–3

My Father,

L-O-V-E! It is my desperate reaching out to share in the depths of another's soul. It is the vulnerable opening of my heart to receive the same tender touch from them.

I always have that fear, deep down inside, that something I do or say will cause the one I love to take back that love and leave me empty, lost, and broken.

And that is how I come to You, God—empty, lost, and broken. My soul cries out to You. Trembling, I open up myself to receive *Your* love to fill my emptiness, to help me find my way, and to put me back together—better, stronger, and fearless in Your presence, the God who created me!

You *are LOVE*! Your love engulfs me completely and freely with no conditions! With trust, simple trust, I humbly open up my soul to You!

My child,

All the painful things, I went through for you. I offered up loud cries with prayers and petitions to My Father, the One who could save Me from death, but He did not. God did hear Me, but I had to die to save you and all My children who would believe. I was reverently submissive, and I learned obedience through the things that I suffered. Once I was made perfect, I became the source of eternal salvation for all who would believe and obey Me.

I hear you cry out when you are suffering. I can save you, but sometimes I do not. I hear your loud cries. I see the injustice. I feel your pain. I see your tears.

Sometimes I allow you to suffer so I can humble you, strengthen you, and use you to bring healing and life to My hurting children. Offer the sufferings up to Me.

I asked My Father to forgive the ones who sinned against Me and hated Me! Ask Him, and He will help you forgive. Some have been blinded by the enemy and do not know what they are doing.

—Hebrews 5:7–8; Luke 23:34

Jesus,

I confess; I spend so much time *doing* and so little time just *being* who You created me to be. I spend so much time talking, planning, worrying, and asking and so little time listening, quietly listening for the sweet sound of Your voice.

I know You want to love me and share Your heart with me.

Oh, sweet Jesus, help me to feel Your love deeply. I want to feel Your presence, see You, hear Your tender whispers above the clamor of my busyness. May Your Words be sealed in my heart. May I listen for Your still, small whisper, calling me to come and just sit at Your feet.

I obey! Here I quietly sit at Your feet. I feel Your sweet breath on my cheek as You whisper in my ear, "I love you, My child!" The love in Your eyes erases all the fear and doubt from my soul.

Our hearts unite as one. Your desire has been fulfilled—the Father, You; Jesus; the Holy Spirit; *and me!*—a true *miracle*!

My child,

I am near you. I am touching you. My Spirit is moving all around you in the wings of the wind. That wind touches your cheek gently. *Feel* Me!

The birds are singing their sweet songs! *Hear* Me!

In indescribable beauty, the flowers are reaching up their petals! *See* Me! In perfect harmony, everything is praising Me! Listen to the Words!

In your weakness, I am strength!

In your disappointments, I am hope! In your pain, I am joy!

In the silence, I am your song!

In your confusion, I am peace! *I AM...*

—2 Corinthians 12:10; Psalm 71:5; John 15:11; Psalm 32:7; John 20:19

Thank You, God…

 …that You are here with me in this moment. I don't have to rush through this day but can enjoy Your presence in this moment…in *every* moment!
 You are *love*.
 You are *joy*.
 You are *peace*.
 You are my heart's desire!
 How often am I quiet enough to hear Your footsteps as You walk into the room?
 How often do I take the time to just enjoy a moment with You? And You are in my *every* moment!
 Oh, my Father, draw my heart and mind away from all the empty things that shout for my attention.
 May I simply revel in the beauty of You—yes, You, only *You*!

My child,

I see you wherever you are. I know you wherever you are. I am with you wherever you are.

Pause in the stillness, and let your heart become one with Mine. Drop the worries and cares at the foot of My cross. Don't let them choke out My life within you!

In the midst of this life, I am your peace!

In the midst of this life, I am your strength! In the midst of this life, I am your life!

You have the power by My Spirit to handle any and every situation that comes your way! Walk in the light of My presence. There is no trace of darkness in Me!

I am your all-powerful and awesome God! *Nothing* is too hard for Me!

—Matthew 28:20; Isaiah 41:10; Psalm
73:26; Psalm 89:15; Jeremiah 32:17

Dear Jesus,

Sometimes, many times, I just want to ask, "Why?"

Why should a beautiful person, who has not had a chance to live fully, be suddenly ripped away from us? We are left with deep, deep pain and agonizing emptiness!

Why would my soulmate be taken from me in the saddest of ways, leaving me to live with one-half of myself?

I think, *How dare I ask why of the Creator of the universe, the One who gave His life for me?*

And then You remind me; You also asked, "*Why?*"— "*My* God, My God, *why* have You forsaken Me?"

You knew pain of all pain. You were forsaken by those You loved dearly! You lost friends and family that were dear to You! You carried on! You kept going one step at a time! You had to face the deepest of all pain and agony…and You felt alone!

But after the *why*, You cried, "Into Thy hands, I commit My Spirit!" So *His hands* were still there!

So into those same *hands*, I commit the deepness of my loneliness, my emptiness, my pain, my destiny, and my wondering why.

Yes, even when I feel alone, the Father's hands are right here! The Father's hands will always be!

My child,

Yes, I heard you calling to Me in desperation. I saw the pain and hurt hanging heavy on your heart. I heard your gasp. I knew its dreadful weight was tearing you apart!

Step back a bit in time, and *look at Me!* There, on the cross, *your* pain and hurt hung heavy on *My* heart! Its dreadful weight was tearing *Me* apart, and I died there *for you!*

So come and kneel at the foot of My cross. Just *look at Me!* Drop this heavy burden. There is no need to carry it. I died for *all of this* so long ago!

Look at Me! You are free!

—Isaiah 53:4-5; John 8:36

Jesus,

I am so grateful for the way You have taken care of me in the past and for Your tender care for me now. You always hold me close. You are the One who dries my tears. You touch my soul in the deepest part.

You prepare the way ahead of me. I'm following step-by-step. Sometimes it is one faltering step at a time.

You hold my hand when the world says we can't touch, hold, or embrace. In the world, it is all about fear. You touch me, hold me, and embrace me with *no* fear or regret. There is no safer place for me to be but in Your arms!

You speak peace in the midst of my raging waters. In Your presence, I am still, not rushed. I am quiet and at peace!

Sometimes You meet us in the small, the hardly visible. Open my eyes that I may see more of You in the silent—the simple—the uncluttered.

Worry? You know not the word!

Here in Your presence, I wait! Here in Your presence, I adore! Come, let us all adore You!

My child,

I am *big* enough to hold you in the palm of My hand. I am *strong* enough to lift you up in each moment of weakness. I am *powerful* enough to accomplish all My purposes in you and through you. I am *wise* enough to design each pathway I desire for you to follow.

I am *holy* enough to melt away the stains of sin, to wash them from you. I am *pure* enough to lead you in the paths of righteousness.

I am *loving* enough to hold you close and heal all the pain that stains your soul. I am *gentle* enough to pick you up tenderly when you fall and to walk beside you.

I am *awesome* enough to fill your heart and soul with joy!

I am *Light.* I go ahead of you and clear the way. I am *Life.* I speak My words to you to breathe My power into you and give you strength to be all that I plan for you to be—*I AM!*

Listen and *trust*!

—John 8:58; Isaiah 6:3; Proverbs 3:5–6; John 3:16

Dear Jesus,

I don't want You to be sad when You look down on me. I want You to smile and enjoy being with me. In many of the pictures that depict what some think You might look like, You look so very solemn.

Oh, to look upon Your face and see You smile, to hear You laugh in joy and happiness—how great that would be!

I'm sure You smiled when You played with the children! You probably chuckled when Peter asked You to bid him come to You on the water! You surely smiled at the little girl You raised from the dead! I'm sure You smiled when the wedding guests tasted Your water that turned into wine! And I'm sure Your face glowed with happiness when You ascended back into heaven and saw the face of Your Father!

Please smile down on us today! May Your joy fill our hearts always! The joy of the Lord truly is our strength!

My child,

Heaven is full of smiles, laughter, and happiness, and heaven can be anywhere that I am. I promised that I would be with you always, even to the end of the age! I am here!

Joy is light that radiates from My presence. Even if you cannot see Me smile, you can feel the joy! My Holy Spirit plants it within your soul.

The dimensions of joy cannot be described in human terms. There are many you know nothing of.

Your eyes have not seen. Your ears have not heard. It hasn't even entered into your heart the things I am preparing for you because you love Me and have been called to accomplish My purposes, but I am revealing these things to you by My Spirit—even now!

Look… Listen… Receive.

Yes, *I am* smiling down on you!

—Matthew 28:20; 1 Corinthians 2:9–10

From the author:

Prayer is conversing with the living God. We share what is on our hearts. He, in turn, shares His heart with us.

He can speak to us through His Word, perhaps a good book, or even through a friend.

How many times have I been too busy to hear the birds singing or feel the gentle breeze caressing my cheek or just to stop and admire the beauty of a rose? He is speaking!

Sometimes it is that still, small voice deep within… maybe just a whisper!

May we all take the time to step aside from the busy-ness and noise of our daily lives and simply *listen*!

—Joy A. Emery-Gulden

About the Author

Joy became a believer at a very young age. She went forward in a church service, and her father prayed with her to receive Jesus. There was a lot of tension in her home growing up, and her faith was the stronghold she needed.

She grew up in Connecticut and Massachusetts. She graduated from Amherst Regional High School in Amherst, Massachusetts.

After high school, Joy attended Moody Bible Institute in Chicago, Illinois. She graduated with a major in Christian education.

Over the years, Joy has been involved, first and foremost, as a mother to two beautiful daughters and a grandmother to two precious granddaughters. She has been a Girl Scout leader, a Sunday school teacher, a youth club choir director, a preschool teacher, and a Stephen minister. She also worked many years selling insurance and recently retired from the real estate industry.

In 2018, Joy lost her youngest granddaughter, Mykaela, in a car accident. She was fifteen years old. The same year, her husband, John, passed away after battling Alzheimer's disease. After his death, she took a position working as an activity assistant in a nearby Alzheimer's facility. She also became a Eucharistic Minister and was able to bring Holy

Communion to the residents during and after the COVID-19 outbreak.

Joy is now enjoying retirement. She recently married a wonderful man who was a widower.

She trusts that the messages in this book will help bring the hope and healing to others that she has experienced.

ACKNOWLEDGEMENTS

My Heartfelt Thank You to:

- My Lord and Savior, Jesus Christ, who is the total inspiration behind every page of this book, and who gave me the courage to follow through. Thank you!
- Anne Horst, the lovely lady who led the retreat on prayer that I attended. This book would not exist without your encouraging us to LISTEN to what God has to say to us. Thank you!
- Linda Hartzfeld, our assistant minister's wife, you invited me to help you at that retreat, and I was so happy I said, "Yes!" Thank you!
- Charity Wallace and Allison Roden, my two beautiful daughters, and Selah Schneider, my precious granddaughter, you have been my greatest support and encouragement in under-taking this project. Thank you!
- Colman Gulden, my husband, you have supported me and stood beside me all the way! Thank you!
- Lisa Dabramo, you are the one who put my manuscript in correct format for me. Thank you!
- Tony Dabramo, you saved all my manuscript documents and transferred them to my new computer. Thank you!
- Linda Sharp, my wonderful long-time friend, you faithfully persisted in encouraging me to get this work published. Thank you!

- Vern Krieger, you read a first draft and felt it was worthy of publishing. Thank you!
- Linay Lencioni, my manager in real estate, you knew about my goal to finish my book and continually pressed me to keep going. Thank you!
- Donna Krech, CEO and author, years ago, you believed I had the makings of a book in me. Thank you!
- Kevin Springer, retired pastor and author, and your beautiful wife Suzanne, you gave me the courage to pursue the publishing process. Thank you!
- Suzy Carr, you first introduced me to Covenant Books and patiently answered all my questions. Thank you!
- Maureen Kinley, my publishing coordinator, you have been walking beside me each step of the way. Thank you!
- Covenant Books, who accepted my manuscript, and each person there who contributed to the development of this book. Thank you!
- To every one of my readers who will share these insights with me. Thank you!

GOD BLESS YOU ALL!

www.ingramcontent.com/pod-product-compliance
Lightning Source LLC
Chambersburg PA
CBHW051335150726
47997CB00004B/1474